Faith In Action

52 WEEKS OF DRAWING CLOSER TO GOD

Terry "TeeJay" Britton

REJOICE
Essential Publishing

Copyright © 2024 by Terry "TeeJay" Britton

All rights reserved. No part of this publication may be reproduced, distributed or transmitted in any form or by any means, including photocopying, recording, or other electronic or mechanical methods, without the prior written permission of the publisher, except in the case of brief quotations embodied in critical reviews and certain other noncommercial uses permitted by copyright law. For mission requests, write to the publisher, addressed " Attention: Permissions Coordinator," at the address below.

Terry "TeeJay" Britton/Rejoice Essential Publishing
PO BOX 512
Effingham, SC 29541
www.republishing.org

Unless otherwise indicated, scripture is taken from the King James Version.

Scripture quotations marked (NIV) are taken from the Holy Bible, New International Version®, NIV®. Copyright © 1973, 1978, 1984, 2011 by Biblica, Inc.™ Used by permission of Zondervan. All rights reserved worldwide. www.zondervan.com The "NIV" and "New International Version" are trademarks registered in the United States Patent and Trademark Office by Biblica, Inc.™

Scripture taken from the New King James Version®. Copyright © 1982 by Thomas Nelson. Used by permission. All rights reserved.

Faith In Action/Terry "TeeJay" Britton

ISBN-13: 979-8-3483-0783-7

Dedication

I dedicate this book to my Mother Carolyn "Cat Toe" Britton.

TABLE OF CONTENTS

Acknowledgements..vii
Foreword..vii
Introduction...1
Week 1..2
Week 2..4
Week 3..6
Week 4..8
Week 5..10
Week 6..12
Week 7..14
Week 8..16
Week 9..18
Week 10..20
Week 11..22
Week 12..24
Week 13..26
Week 14..28
Week 15..30
Week 16..32
Week 17..34
Week 18..36
Week 19..38
Week 20..40
Week 21..42
Week 22..44
Week 23..46
Week 24..48

Week 25	50
Week 26	52
Week 27	54
Week 28	56
Week 29	58
Week 30	60
Week 31	62
Week 32	64
Week 33	66
Week 34	68
Week 35	70
Week 36	72
Week 37	74
Week 38	76
Week 39	78
Week 40	80
Week 41	82
Week 42	84
Week 43	86
Week 44	88
Week 45	90
Week 46	92
Week 47	94
Week 48	96
Week 49	98
Week 50	100
Week 51	102
Week 52	104
Bonus Week	106
About The Author	108

Acknowledgements

I WOULD LIKE TO acknowledge my wife Britney and kids, who always support me in everything I do.

Thanks to my siblings Raymond, Martessa, Tenisha (Sugar), William (Oldest Brother Mareece (RIH), and my dad Raymond Sr (RIH) for always having my back.

Thanks to my best friend Matt, who ensured I finished what I started.

My friend Terrence, thank you for giving me a mighty word from the Lord that was on time.

Thank you, Pastor Dan and Pastor Cindy Wermuth for faithfully covering me in prayer as I work on my book; your support means so much to me.

Last but not least, thanks to Momma Murdy, who encouraged me over the years to write. She got me my first journal to write my thoughts.

Foreword

I would consider this prayer journal a required reading for every believer to encourage them in their walk with God. **"Faith In Action: 52 Weeks Of Drawing Closer To God"** is a positive tool to enhance one's faith walk. Follow the weekly exercises and write down what the Lord speaks to you.

— Bishop Ron Webb
Mount Calvary Powerhouse Church

Introduction

My biggest prayer for you is that you would know that you are loved so much that God sent his only Son, Jesus Christ, to live a life you couldn't live (perfection), and to pay a price you were meant to pay by His death on the cross as punishment for your sins. And on the third day, He rose from the grave just like He said He would, overcoming sin and death and allowing you to be reconciled to your Heavenly Father for eternity, if you would only accept His sacrifice and believe in Him. He thought you were worth it; your life matters to him. You are loved, and when you don't feel loved, check out John 3:16 to help remind you. I pray that this prayer journal will help each of you who follows Jesus, whether you're young in the faith or have known Him for a long time. I hope you will allow it to be a special place to write your prayers and talk to God about what is on your heart. As you read and pray, allow God to step in and help you to grow and trust Him more. I've found that writing in a journal can make a significant difference in your life and help you feel closer to Him every day. I have prayed over each of these journals that they will be a blessing to you as you continue your walk with Him.

Be blessed, Teejay

Faith In Action

WEEK 1

Finding Your Identity in Christ

Today, I choose not to let other people's opinions or my fear of failure define who I am. In Christ, I am secure and know who I am. Jesus, I will stay close to You and rest in the identity that you have given me. I won't chase after validation from others, and my worth isn't tied to how people see me or what I achieve. I am enough because of who I am in You. Thank You, Lord, for freeing me from the need for approval. Amen!

Reflection Verse:

"Fearing what others think is a trap, but trusting in the Lord brings safety." - Proverbs 29:25 NLT

Journaling Exercise:

Make a list of the roles you play in life —like student, friend, employee, sibling, or leader. Where do you seek approval to feel valued? Do you struggle with feeling unworthy until you receive recognition? Or do the opinions of others hold you back? Spend some prayer time asking God to show why you feel this way. Surrender those insecurities to Him and remind yourself that God's opinion is the one that matters most. No comment, label, or assumption from others can define you. You are God's child—so live confidently in that truth.

NOTES

WEEK 2
Living with Faith

Let the faith of Jesus rise within you today. Faith to heal. Faith to live fully. Faith to manage your finances. Faith to start something new. Faith to stand firm. Faith to ask for help. Faith to show up even when it's hard. Faith to keep going. Faith to get out of bed. Faith to chase a dream. Faith to stop running from what scares you. Faith to trust that God will show up. Faith to give generously. Faith to love deeply. Faith to smile. Faith to laugh. Faith to believe again. Jesus, help us. Amen.

Reflection Verses:

"In fact, this is love for God: to keep his commands. And his commands are not burdensome, for everyone born of God overcomes the world. This is the victory that has overcome the world, even our faith." – 1 John 5:3-4 NIV

Journaling Exercise:

In the Bible, faith can mean both believing and being faithful in action. Sometimes, belief comes first, and our actions follow. Other times, we act in faith even when we don't feel it yet—and over time, our hearts and mindsets catch up. Write down 2-3 areas in your life where you want stronger faith. How can you show faithfulness in those areas, even if you don't feel it right away? Faith grows when we take small, consistent steps, trusting that God will meet us along the way.

Living with Faith

NOTES

WEEK 3
Understanding God's Intentions

May you fully realize how good God's intentions are for you. His plans give life. They are thoughtful, guided by the Holy Spirit, and full of purpose. They build you up. They focus on grace and redemption. They are full of love, hope, and lasting impact. His plans create growth and bear good fruit. They are eternal, always moving toward something greater. And at the center of it all is Jesus. Amen.

Reflection Verses:

"For God so loved the world that he gave his one and only Son, that whoever believes in him shall not perish but have eternal life. For God did not send his Son into the world to condemn the world, but to save the world through him." – John 3:16-17 NIV

Exercise: Reading and Reflection

In these verses, God reveals that Jesus came not to judge us, but to save us. Salvation isn't just about getting to heaven—it's about knowing God personally and experiencing His life-changing power in every part of our lives. Take a moment to read the scriptures above twice, thinking of it as God's personal message to you. Let it remind you of how He sees you and what He desires for your future.

NOTES

WEEK 4
Igniting Heavenly Passions

Pray today that God's passions spark within you. May His purpose for your life ignite like a fire—filling you, working through you, and spreading around you, today and always. Amen!

Reflection Verse:

"So whether you eat or drink or whatever you do, do it all for the glory of God." –1 Corinthians 10:31 NIV

Exercise: Prayer and Action

Passion for God's work can start in prayer, but it grows through action. Ask God how He wants you to spend your time today.

- Do you need to sit quietly and connect with Him?
- Is there someone on your heart you should share your faith with?
- Have you taken time to worship lately?
- Could you use some time reading and reflecting on Scripture?
- Is there a local outreach or cause where you could volunteer?

Listen for God's direction—and then act on it.

NOTES

FAITH IN ACTION

WEEK 5

The Light of Christ

Today, pray that the light of Jesus shines into any dark areas of your life. May His light help you move forward again. May fear lose its grip on you, and anything that tries to intimidate you be silenced. Let sin, sickness, and the enemy's plans be uncovered, so you can make choices that lead to life, goodness, and growth. As you go through your day, may you also spread that light to others—driving out fear, exposing lies, and bringing hope wherever you go. Light to you. Hope to you. Jesus to you. Amen!

Reflection Verses:

"In him was life, and that life was the light of all mankind. The light shines in the darkness, and the darkness has not overcome it." – John 1:4-5 NIV

Exercise: Share the Light

Jesus is the light that brings life to everyone. Today, think about how you would explain the Gospel—what God has done through Jesus—in your own words. Write down a short version of it:
- How has God worked through Jesus?
- What does that mean for your life and for others?

If you can, talk about your thoughts with another believer or mentor. Then, try sharing what you've written with someone today. It could be a friend or someone you meet by chance. Record any important points from your conversations and reflect on what you learn through these discussions.

NOTES

WEEK 6
Finding Peace

Today, pray that everything in your life that feels chaotic, unpredictable, or stressful will be calmed by the One who is never anxious or confused. May the unchanging God—the one who holds all things good, right, and peaceful—fill you with His peace today and overflow it into every part of your life. Amen!

Reflection Verses:

"Your eyes saw my unformed body; all the days ordained for me were written in your book before one of them came to be. How precious to me are your thoughts, God! How vast is the sum of them! Were I to count them, they would outnumber the grains of sand—when I awake, I am still with you." – Psalm 139:16-18 NIV

Exercise: Reflecting on Psalm 139

Take some time to read all of Psalm 139 slowly. Let David's words be your own prayer, especially for the areas of your life that feel overwhelming or uncertain.

Remember: God has already mapped out every day of your life, and nothing surprises Him. As you pray through this Psalm, sit in God's presence and listen as He speaks peace over you. Let His truth calm your heart and remind you that He is with you every step of the way.

NOTES

FAITH IN ACTION

WEEK 7

Finding Peace with Yourself

Today, pray for healing—healing between you and yourself. May you reconnect with the real you—the joyful, vibrant, fully alive version of yourself. The you that existed before the mistakes, the pain, the things that hurt you or made you feel lost. You've carried shame long enough; today is the day to lift your head and let it go! In Jesus' name, shame has no hold on you. Lift your eyes and see Jesus reaching for you—He's smiling, maybe even laughing, as He offers grace and makes you new. Stop punishing yourself. We've all fallen short, but Jesus has already dealt with it. His grace stretches far and reaches even you. Be healed and free today, and share that freedom with the world around you. Amen!

Reflection Verse:

"Let the peace of Christ rule in your hearts, since as members of one body you were called to peace. And be thankful."
— Colossians 3:15 NIV

Exercise: Reflection and Meditation

If you can, find a mirror. Look into your own eyes for about 20 seconds. How do you feel looking at yourself? Is it hard to make eye contact? Do you see only your past mistakes? Jesus came so that you could experience peace—even within yourself. When we embrace His peace, we reflect His love and power to the world around us. If you don't feel at peace with yourself today, ask yourself why. Be brutally honest: What words come to mind when you think about yourself? Write them down. Then sit quietly and ask God to show you which thoughts reflect His truth and which don't. Let Him speak to your heart, and write down what you hear.

NOTES

WEEK 8

The Power of Prayer

Today, I hope you recognize the incredible power of prayer. It's not just a routine or habit—it's a real connection to eternity. Through prayer, God's power flows through us here on earth. It's an opportunity to be with the Creator and take part in His redemptive plan for the world. May your heart come alive as you experience this connection with heaven. Amen!

Reflection Verses:

"This, then, is how you should pray: 'Our Father in heaven, hallowed be your name, your kingdom come, your will be done, on earth as it is in heaven. Give us today our daily bread. And forgive us our debts, as we also have forgiven our debtors. And lead us not into temptation, but deliver us from the evil one.'" – Matthew 6:9-13 NIV

Exercise: Meditation and Prayer

Picture Jesus teaching His followers about prayer. The Lord's Prayer is more than just words to memorize—it's a way to connect with God and align with His heart. Many traditions use this prayer in slightly different ways, but its beauty lies in its simplicity and meaning. First, read the Lord's Prayer straight through as a prayer to God. Then, read it again, slowly and out loud. Pause after each line to reflect on what it means. For example, "Your will be done, on earth as it is in heaven." — What does it look like for God's will to be done in your life today? "Forgive us our debts."—Is there anything you need to ask forgiveness for? Ask the Holy Spirit to help you experience the depth of this prayer. Someone taught me this. To stay connected throughout your day, keep a small object—like a rock or coin—in your pocket. Whenever you notice or touch it, pause and say the Lord's Prayer again. Use it as a reminder of your time with God and reflect on what He showed you.

NOTES

Faith In Action

WEEK 9
A Clear Mind

Pray that your mind becomes clear and calm today. May peace and clarity take over your thoughts. Anxiety, distractions, and anything that tries to overwhelm you—let them lose their grip. In the name of Jesus, who brings peace to our minds, I pray for freedom and focus. Amen!

Reflection Verse:

"Do not conform to the pattern of this world, but be transformed by the renewing of your mind. Then you will be able to test and approve what God's will is—His good, pleasing, and perfect will." – Romans 12:2 NIV

Exercise: Journaling for Clarity

Take a moment to write down everything that's on your mind. Include both positive and negative thoughts, as well as any neutral things that are taking up space.
- Are certain thoughts making you feel restless or anxious?
- Are there things on your mind that bring joy or peace?

Once you've written everything down, reflect on each thought. Which ones align with God's truth, and which ones don't? Pray over all of it—ask the Holy Spirit to take the weight of your thoughts and bring you clarity and peace. Surrender both the good and the bad, and listen for any direction or insight God gives you.

A Clear Mind

NOTES

WEEK 10
Letting Go of Pride

Jesus, save me from myself—that's your prayer today. Help me stop acting like everything revolves around me. You are the reason I live, move, and exist. Your Word says that You hold everything together, so remind me that I'm here for Your glory, not my own. I let go of pride and selfish goals today. I want my life to be about You as I follow Your example and carry my cross daily. Amen.

Reflection Verses:

"Then he said to them all: "Whoever wants to be my disciple must deny themselves and take up their cross daily and follow me. For whoever wants to save their life will lose it, but whoever loses their life for me will save it. What good is it for someone to gain the whole world, and yet lose or forfeit their very self?" – Luke 9:23-25 NIV

Exercise: Journaling and Reflection

Who is Jesus to you? Take some time to write down how you see Him. Think back to when you first gave your life to Him. Why did you make that decision? What stood out to you about His love, grace, or sacrifice?

Don't rush through this—remind yourself of how good God is and how deeply He loves you. Remember that your life is meant to reflect His glory, not your own. He is Lord, and any goodness or greatness in us comes from living in His light. Use this journaling time to re-center your heart and align it with His purpose.

NOTES

WEEK 11
Thankful For His Grace

Jesus, You've saved me from myself and given me more grace than I could ever mess up. I know I'll make mistakes—sometimes a lot in one day—but Your grace is always bigger than my failures. Even when I'm selfish or thoughtless, Your grace waits patiently, meets me in my brokenness, and restores me. Thank You for letting me know that no matter how far I fall, I'll never be beyond Your reach. Help me never take Your grace for granted. Amen!

Reflection Verses:

"For it is by grace you have been saved, through faith—and this is not from yourselves, it is the gift of God—not by works, so that no one can boast." – Ephesians 2:8-9 NIV

Exercise: Prayer and Reflection

Grace means receiving what we don't deserve—God's love, forgiveness, and favor. When you choose Jesus, His sacrifice covers all your past, present, and future mistakes. Nothing can separate you from His love. Take a few minutes to talk with God through prayer. Write down your thoughts:
- Ask for forgiveness in any area of your life where you haven't fully trusted or followed Him.
- Thank Him for the endless grace that covers you every day.

Let today be a reminder that His love isn't based on your performance—it's a gift that never runs out.

NOTES

Faith In Action

WEEK 12

Standing Against the Enemy

Stay sharp today—keep your mind and heart alert. Just as God has good plans for you, the enemy's goal is to steal, kill, and destroy. I pray that you recognize his schemes before they take root and do everything you can to stop them. Fight back with prayer, kindness, and action that advances God's kingdom. Be empowered by the Holy Spirit today and trust in His strength. Amen!

Reflection Verse:

"No weapon forged against you will prevail, and you will refute every tongue that accuses you. This is the heritage of the servants of the Lord, and this is their vindication from me," declares the Lord.
—Isaiah 54:17 NIV

Exercise: Journaling, Prayer, and Accountability

Take 5 minutes to sit quietly with a pen and paper.
- Write down any areas in your life where you've felt spiritual attack or struggled in the past.
- How can you resist these attacks moving forward?

Our battle isn't against people but against spiritual forces. God has given us His Spirit to fight with wisdom and power. If you face stress or conflict, memorize a verse about God's peace. If you struggle with fear or doubt, reach out to a trusted friend to pray with you and offer support. For habits or temptations you want to overcome, make a plan ahead of time—set boundaries, avoid triggers, and lean on someone you trust for accountability. We overcome by trusting in what Jesus has done and by sharing how God works in our lives. You don't fight alone—God is with you, and your brothers and sisters in Christ are too. Today is a fresh start.

NOTES

WEEK 13
Purify Me, Cleanse Me

God, this is my prayer today. Please purify my thoughts, motives, and plans. Help me to be real—transparent and honest, not pretending or hiding behind religious words. Make me someone who reflects who Jesus truly is, not just going through the motions of faith. Holy Spirit, I ask You to lead and change me from the inside out. Amen and amen.

Reflection Verses:

"*Create in me a clean heart, O God.*" – Psalm 51:10

"*Have mercy on me, O God, according to your unfailing love; according to your great compassion blot out my transgressions. Wash away all my iniquity and cleanse me from my sin.*" - Psalm 51:1-2 NIV

Exercise: Reading and Prayer

1. Read Psalm 51 slowly and thoughtfully.
2. As you read, ask God to reveal any areas in your life where your heart has been off track—where pride, selfishness, or complacency have taken root.
3. Pray for God to cleanse your heart, not just so you'll feel better, but so you can live authentically in His love and show it to others.

Ask God for specific ways you can reveal His heart to the people around you today. Make it about Him, not your own reputation. Trust that He will give you opportunities to reflect His grace for His glory alone.

NOTES

WEEK 14
God Is Smiling At You

Please know that God is smiling at you. Even if it doesn't feel that way, He is. He's not angry or keeping score of every mistake you make. God isn't waiting to punish you like a strict officer handing out tickets. Instead, He is a redeemer, a healer, and a reconciler. His biggest smile toward you is Jesus—through Christ's resurrection, God shows how much He loves and accepts you. When you accept Jesus, God sees you through Him, not through your failures. Live in His love and acceptance today. Amen!

Reflection Verses:

"If anyone acknowledges that Jesus is the Son of God, God lives in them and they in God. And so we know and rely on the love God has for us. God is love. Whoever lives in love lives in God, and God in them. This is how love is made complete among us so that we will have confidence on the day of judgment: In this world, we are like Jesus. There is no fear in love. But perfect love drives out fear, because fear has to do with punishment. The one who fears is not made perfect in love. We love because He first loved us." – 1 John 4:15-19 NIV

Exercise: Silence and Meditation

Sometimes, we feel like we have to perform to earn God's approval, thinking we aren't enough or that He's disappointed in us. But your identity isn't based on what you do—it's rooted in what Christ has already done for you. Take 10-15 minutes to sit quietly before God, and maybe play worship music softly in the background. Ask Him to show you how He sees you. Read today's passage slowly, as many times as needed. Let His love sink in and replace any fear or anxiety. Rest in knowing that God smiles at you, simply because He loves you.

NOTES

WEEK 15

Prayer For Discernment And Peace

Pray this prayer today. Holy Spirit, I'm asking you to sharpen my discernment. May the things that feel unclear or confusing become crystal clear. Where I feel overwhelmed or stuck in grey areas, let there be clarity. May any anxiety weighing on me be replaced with shalom—the deep peace that only comes from God. Jesus, help me experience Your rest, not just in theory, but in real life. Thank You for going ahead of me today. May Your will guide my actions, and may Your kingdom show up in my life. Amen.

Reflection Verse:

"But the Advocate, the Holy Spirit, whom the Father will send in my name, will teach you all things and will remind you of everything I have said to you." – John 14:26 NIV

Exercise: Journaling

Do you feel lost or confused in any area of your life right now? Pray today's prayer over yourself and anyone else who needs clarity. Take a few moments to journal your thoughts. Write down your prayer and invite the Holy Spirit to guide you. Pay attention to what comes to mind as you listen—God still speaks today. Trust that the Holy Spirit is active and working, bringing you discernment, peace, and strength to live for God's glory.

NOTES

FAITH IN ACTION

WEEK 16
A Fire in Your Heart

This morning, ask God to spark a fire in your soul—a flame that burns bright and steady. May His presence fill you in such a way that others can feel the warmth and hope through your words and actions. May you encounter Jesus more deeply today, and may others be drawn to Him through the love and light in you. Amen.

Reflection Verse:

"But we have this treasure in jars of clay to show that this all-surpassing power is from God and not from us." — 2 Corinthians 4:7 NIV

Exercise: Prayer and Service

Ask God to give you opportunities to step outside your comfort zone today. Be open to displaying His love in ways that go beyond what you can do on your own. Look for moments to love others selflessly, serve in meaningful ways, and offer encouragement to someone who might need it. Make it a point to engage deeper with one family member or close friend—someone you haven't really connected with lately. Pray for the Holy Spirit to guide your words and actions so that your time together reflects the love and power of Christ.

A Fire in Your Heart

NOTES

Faith In Action

WEEK 17

His Presence in Your Life

Today, pray that you notice clear signs of God's presence around you. He promised that He is with us, and His presence is all the proof we need. Be aware of the ways God might be showing Himself in your everyday life—whether through a kind word, a moment of peace, or an unexpected blessing. Enjoy these moments with Him, and use them as opportunities to point others toward our personal, loving God. Amen.

Reflection Verse:

"They triumphed over him by the blood of the Lamb and by the word of their testimony; they did not love their lives so much as to shrink from death." – Revelation 12:11 NIV

Exercise: Prayer and Evangelism

Build on the work God started in you yesterday. Ask the Holy Spirit to help you stay focused on Jesus, no matter where you are—at school, work, or home. Pray for opportunities to see Christ working in those around you and for boldness to speak life into their situations. Step out in faith with words of encouragement, love, or even just a listening ear. Seek to love others without expecting anything in return, giving all the credit to God. Today, be intentional in sharing the hope of Jesus with someone—whether through a conversation, an act of kindness, or simply being present in their life.

NOTES

WEEK 18

Breaking Out of Complacency

Pray that you would feel a spark within yourself today, stirring you out of complacency. May God move you beyond comfort and into purpose, calling you to live boldly for His Kingdom. Let His will be done in and through you today. May selfishness and distractions fall away, making room for a heart fully focused on Him. Amen.

Reflection Verses:

"Do you not know that in a race all the runners run, but only one gets the prize? Run in such a way as to get the prize. Everyone who competes in the games goes into strict training. They do it to get a crown that will not last, but we do it to get a crown that will last forever. Therefore I do not run like someone running aimlessly; I do not fight like a boxer beating the air. No, I strike a blow to my body and make it my slave so that after I have preached to others, I myself will not be disqualified for the prize." – 1 Corinthians 9:24-27 NIV

Exercise: Journaling and Reflection

Complacency sneaks in when we get too comfortable, losing sight of God's purpose for us. Spend some quiet time asking the Holy Spirit to show you areas where you've become stuck in routine or have focused too much on yourself. Are there moments where you've overlooked opportunities to serve others or neglected what God is calling you to? Write down what comes to mind—whether it's attitudes, habits, or situations. Be honest with yourself, and where necessary, repent. Ask God for strength to grow in these areas, and commit to living an intentional and sacrificial life, pressing forward for the prize that lasts forever.

NOTES

Faith In Action

WEEK 19

Fear's Fear

Pray that God would calm your fears today. May He remind you that fear is afraid of Him. May you witness your fears tremble, shrink, and disappear in His presence—and as you experience freedom, may the same happen for those around you. Amen.

Reflection Verse:

"Have I not commanded you? Be strong and courageous. Do not be afraid; do not be discouraged, for the LORD your God will be with you wherever you go." – Joshua 1:9 NIV

Exercise: Meditation and Prayer

When God told Joshua to be strong and courageous, it wasn't because Joshua had to rely on his own strength or bravery. Joshua could move forward boldly because God was with him every step of the way. The true hero of that story—and ours—is God, not us.

Take a few minutes to sit quietly with today's verse. Reflect on moments in your life where fear has held you back, and think of people around you who may be facing fear right now. Pray that God's presence will encourage and guide them. Ask Him to replace fear with His peace, both in your heart and theirs.

NOTES

FAITH IN ACTION

WEEK 20
Living As The New You

Live like the new creation you are. Stop dragging around the old, worn-out version of yourself—the one filled with shame, fear, or hopelessness. That person no longer defines you. Because of what Jesus accomplished, you are new. Let go of the past, and step into the life that reflects who you are now.

Reflection Verses:

"Forget the former things; do not dwell on the past. See, I am doing a new thing! Now it springs up; do you not perceive it? I am making a way in the wilderness and streams in the wasteland." – Isaiah 43:18-19 NIV

Exercise: Prayer and Reflection

Jesus came so you could experience life in abundance, not live under the weight of old mistakes or struggles. He isn't frustrated or disappointed in you—His love is real, and He's fiercely opposed to anything that holds you back. Take a few minutes to think about what might be keeping you from fully living in the new life God offers. Is there fear, hurt, or unhealthy patterns getting in the way? Whether Jesus brings change instantly or through a journey, surrender those things to Him today. Ask Him to take control, guide you, and remind you of who you are—a beloved child of God, walking in freedom.

NOTES

WEEK 21
Seeing Jesus In Your Day

Today, pray that you'll experience a moment so meaningful you'll know without a doubt that it was Jesus—not luck or coincidence. He is Lord of everything, working in your life, and He wants to draw you closer to Himself. Don't let doubt get in the way. Be refreshed and encouraged as you encounter Him today.

Reflection Verses:

"And let us run with perseverance the race marked out for us, fixing our eyes on Jesus, the pioneer and perfecter of faith. For the joy set before him he endured the cross, scorning its shame, and sat down at the right hand of the throne of God. Consider him who endured such opposition from sinners, so that you will not grow weary and lose heart." – Hebrews 12:1-3 NIV

Exercise: Reflection and Prayer

Hebrews tells us that Jesus willingly faced the suffering of the cross because He knew the joy waiting on the other side—a restored relationship with you. Let that sink in: you were part of His joy. Take 10 minutes to sit quietly and reflect on this truth. Whether you've been following Jesus for years or are just beginning your journey, come back to the cross today. Let His love and sacrifice become real to you again. Ask the Holy Spirit to help you see the beauty of what Jesus has done. Stay in that moment of awe, and let it reignite your passion to follow Him.

NOTES

Faith In Action

WEEK 22

Finding Peace By Still Waters

Jesus, I ask that You guide us to places of rest and peace—those still waters where we can catch our breath. Help us not only find peace for ourselves but also show others how to step into that quiet place with You. Go ahead of me, my family, and my friends today so Your love is reflected in everything we do. Give us rest and trust in You. Amen.

Reflection Verses:

"He stilled the storm to a whisper; the waves of the sea were hushed. They were glad when it grew calm, and he guided them to their desired haven. Let them give thanks to the Lord for his unfailing love and his wonderful deeds for mankind. Let them exalt him in the assembly of the people and praise him in the council of the elders." – Psalm 107:29-32 NIV

Exercise: Meditation and Quiet Reflection

Take a few moments to read Psalm 107:29-32 aloud, slowly and intentionally, focusing on each word. After reading, sit quietly for a minute, inviting God to speak to you in the stillness. Repeat the reading two more times, allowing God's peace to fill you. As you experience that peace, pray the same over the people in your life today, trusting that God will calm any storms they may be facing.

NOTES

FAITH IN ACTION

WEEK 23
Peace In Every Area

May the peace of heaven settle into every part of your life today. Peace over your relationships, finances, health, emotions, thoughts—every area where stress or worry tries to creep in. Amen!

Reflection Verse:

"Now may the Lord of peace himself give you peace at all times and in every way. The Lord be with all of you." — 1 Thessalonians 3:16 NIV

Exercise: Prayer and Reflection

Take a moment to reflect on each area mentioned—relationships, finances, body, emotions, and mind. Slowly read the verse out loud, focusing on one area at a time, asking Jesus to bring His peace and guidance there. Release control of these things to Him in prayer, and trust His direction for your life moving forward.

NOTES

FAITH IN ACTION

WEEK 24

Reconciliation

Today, may God help you rebuild relationships that have been broken by hurt or offense. May the One who heals hearts work in you, giving you the strength to overcome bitterness and pain so you can walk in unity and peace. In Jesus' name, let it be so. Amen!

Reflection Verses:

"So from now on we regard no one from a worldly point of view. Though we once regarded Christ in this way, we do so no longer. Therefore, if anyone is in Christ, the new creation has come: The old has gone, the new is here! All this is from God, who reconciled us to himself through Christ and gave us the ministry of reconciliation: that God was reconciling the world to himself in Christ, not counting people's sins against them. And he has committed to us the message of reconciliation. We are therefore Christ's ambassadors, as though God were making his appeal through us. We implore you on Christ's behalf: Be reconciled to God." – 2 Corinthians 5:16-20 NIV

Exercise: Prayer and Reflection

Reconciliation begins with forgiveness, which often takes time and intentional effort. Spend a few minutes in prayer, asking the Holy Spirit to reveal anyone you need to forgive or reconcile with. Forgiveness is a choice to release the weight of hurt—whether or not you feel ready, the Holy Spirit will help you take the first step. Surrender the situation to God, trust Him to guide you through the process, and remember that forgiveness frees both you and the other person to walk in peace.

NOTES

WEEK 25
Praying For Others' Salvation

Today, pray for the people you care about to experience the kind of life-changing relationship with God that only He can bring. God, send people into their lives—friends, family, or even strangers—who will encourage and inspire them. Use Your Spirit to help them feel Your love, understand Your truth, and be drawn closer to You. I also pray that anything trying to hold them back from knowing You would lose its power. I believe salvation is already at work and will continue to unfold! Amen.

Reflection Verse:

"No one can come to me unless the Father who sent me draws them, and I will raise them up at the last day." – John 6:44 NIV

Action: Pray for Others

God is the one who opens people's hearts to faith, and He works in many ways—whether that's through life events or the people around them. It's not all on you to make things happen. In fact, Jesus cares even more than you do about those you love coming to know Him. So, take time today to pray for them. Trust that God is already working in their hearts, even in ways you might not see. Ask Him to reach them in ways that connect with who they are, and be encouraged—He is drawing them closer step by step.

Praying For Others' Salvation

NOTES

Faith In Action

WEEK 26

Praying For Peace In Every Area

God, help me be someone who brings Your peace wherever I go. I want to experience and share Your peace—in my home, at school, at work, in my city, and in the world. Jesus, You are the ultimate source of real peace, and we need You. Teach us to look to You, the Prince of Peace, so that Your presence can influence every part of life. May Your peace take root in me and flow into the world around me. Amen.

Reflection Verses:

"I urge, then, first of all, that petitions, prayers, intercession and thanksgiving be made for all people—for kings and all those in authority, that we may live peaceful and quiet lives in all godliness and holiness. This is good, and pleases God our Savior, who wants all people to be saved and to come to a knowledge of the truth."— 1 Timothy 2:1-4 NIV

Action: Pray and Journal

Prayer has the power to change things. Today, take a few moments to pray for peace in key areas of your life and beyond. Write down specific people or groups you want to lift up in prayer for each category:

- Home
- School
- Work
- City
- World

As you pray, ask God to bring peace to these places and to use your life to reflect His peace to others. Pray that through this peace, people would come to know God's love more deeply. Take your time journaling these prayers—sometimes writing helps us see where God is already working and reminds us to trust in His plan.

NOTES

WEEK 27

Praying For Total Healing

Today, pray for healing in every part of your life—your body, mind, and spirit. I believe you can experience complete freedom and wholeness. Yes, healing and freedom are yours. Amen.

Reflection Verses:

"Now the Lord is the Spirit, and where the Spirit of the Lord is, there is freedom. And we all, who with unveiled faces reflect the Lord's glory, are being transformed into His image with ever-increasing glory, which comes from the Lord, who is the Spirit." – 2 Corinthians 3:17-18 NIV

Action: Pray for Healing

The kind of freedom Jesus offers brings healing in every area—relationships, physical health, emotions, and spiritual well-being. While complete wholeness will come when we're with Him forever, we can start experiencing it here and now.

Take a moment to reflect on this verse. Let God's strength, hope, love, and peace fill you. Speak the verse over your own life, and ask God for the healing you need. Then, think of one or two people you care about, and pray the same verse over them. Trust that God is already working in their lives, bringing freedom and healing in His time and way.

NOTES

FAITH IN ACTION

WEEK 28

Life Isn't About You

As followers of Jesus, life isn't just about our comfort, preferences, or opinions. It's about God's purpose and plan. Real freedom comes when we recognize this and surrender our ways to Him. He is God—we are not. When we embrace that truth, we can stop stressing over control and focus on living for Him. Amen.

Reflection Verses:

"For my thoughts are not your thoughts, neither are your ways my ways," declares the Lord. "As the heavens are higher than the earth, so are my ways higher than your ways and my thoughts than your thoughts." — Isaiah 55:8-9 NIV

Action: Reflect and Pray

Take a moment to think about any areas of your life that may have become self-focused—maybe without even realizing it. Are there decisions, relationships, or responsibilities you've tried to handle on your own? Spend 5 minutes reflecting on these things.

Ask Jesus for forgiveness for trying to manage them apart from Him. Surrender these areas back to God and listen for His guidance. Trust that His plan is greater than yours, and let that truth set you free to live with purpose today.

NOTES

FAITH IN ACTION

WEEK 29

Listening For God's Voice

Father, speak to me today. I know You are always speaking, even when I'm unaware, but help me hear You clearly now. I'm making space for You. This time is Yours. I sit here with You, ready to listen. Amen.

Reflection Verses:

"My son, if you accept my words and store up my commands within you, turning your ear to wisdom and applying your heart to understanding—indeed, if you call out for insight and cry aloud for understanding, and if you look for it as for silver and search for it as for hidden treasure, then you will understand the fear of the Lord and find the knowledge of God." – Proverbs 2:1-5

Action: Quiet Time and Journaling

Find a quiet spot and grab a pen and paper. Take a few minutes to slow down—breathe in deeply, imagining you're breathing in God's peace, and as you exhale, let go of any stress or distractions. Spend 7-10 minutes in silence, just being with God. If thoughts, people, or situations come to mind, write them down. Ask God what He wants to show you about these areas. If nothing specific comes up, that's okay—just enjoy being in His presence. Listening isn't always about words; sometimes it's about resting with Him and knowing He's near.

NOTES

Faith In Action

WEEK 30
The Power Of Faithfulness

May you experience amazing results through everyday, ordinary actions. The small things you do—like a mustard seed—can grow into something huge. Simple acts of consistency can spark something powerful, like a wildfire for God's Kingdom. May God help you see the value in staying faithful, even when it feels small or unnoticed. Amen.

Reflection Verse:

"Whoever can be trusted with very little can also be trusted with much, and whoever is dishonest with very little will also be dishonest with much." – Luke 16:10 NIV

Action: Reflect and Journal

Take a moment to reflect on what God has placed in your life right now. What responsibilities, relationships, or jobs are you working on in this season? Are you showing up with care and excellence, even in the small things?

Ask the Holy Spirit to guide your thoughts as you reflect on these questions. Write down what comes to mind. Faithfulness in the little things today can open doors to bigger things tomorrow.

NOTES

Faith In Action

WEEK 31

A Holy Fire

Today, pray that God's fire will ignite in your heart. May His Spirit stir those flames to burn away anything holding you back and bring warmth to the cold places in your life. Let His fire purify, renew, and move you forward. God, burn in us today! Amen.

Reflection Verses:

"Be careful not to forget the covenant of the Lord your God that He made with you; do not make for yourselves an idol in the form of anything the Lord your God has forbidden. For the Lord your God is a consuming fire, a jealous God."– Deuteronomy 4:23-24 NIV

Action: Reflect and Meditate

Think about what a fire is like—maybe you've sat around a campfire with friends or family before. Take a moment to close your eyes and picture those flames dancing. If you can, light a candle or sit by a fireplace (safely and legally) and watch the fire for 5-10 minutes.

As you sit quietly, ask God how He wants to work like a fire in your life. What does He want to purify or renew in you? Take this time to slow down, listen, and reflect with Jesus. Sometimes, just sitting in His presence is enough to feel the warmth of His love and direction.

A Holy Fire

NOTES

FAITH IN ACTION

WEEK 32
Mercy And Grace

Today, pray that any hurt or offense you've experienced will be transformed into a deep well of grace within you. May you be surrounded by grace, filled with it, and share it freely. No wound or frustration will be able to hold power over you—they will be flooded and washed away by the overwhelming grace of God. I pray this over your life through the power of the Holy Spirit. Amen.

Reflection Verses:

"The mouth of the righteous is a fountain of life, but the mouth of the wicked conceals violence. Hatred stirs up conflict, but love covers all wrongs." – Proverbs 10:11-12 NIV

Action: Reflect and Journal

Think about recent moments where you felt hurt, offended, or frustrated—whether by people or situations. Write them down in your journal.

Bring each of these moments to God in prayer. Ask the Holy Spirit to guide your response and remind you of who you are in Christ. Release these feelings to Him and invite His grace to flow through you. Let His love replace bitterness, helping you respond with peace and kindness, even when it's hard.

NOTES

WEEK 33
Listening For God's Voice

Holy Spirit, I know You are always speaking, even when it feels quiet. Help me hear You clearly. Teach me how to be patient and wait on You. Amen.

Reflection Verse:

"Be still, and know that I am God; I will be exalted among the nations, I will be exalted in the earth." – Psalm 46:10 NIV

Action: Silence and Meditation

Today, focus on simply being in God's presence—not on getting answers or solutions. Those things will come in time. Instead, use this moment to grow in your understanding of who God is. Find a quiet place where you can avoid distractions. Open your Bible to Psalm 46:10. If possible, take a humble posture, like kneeling. Read the verse out loud slowly. Take a deep breath in, then breathe out. Read it again.

Continue this pattern for 5 to 10 minutes. As you breathe and repeat the verse, reflect on what it means to be still before God. What might it look like for you to fully trust Him today? How can you respond to His greatness? Let these thoughts guide your meditation.

Listening For God's Voice

NOTES

WEEK 34

Praying For Those You Love

Lord Jesus, I lift up my loved ones to You today. I ask that Your peace, hope, love, and strength would surround them in every way. Guide their footsteps, their thoughts and their tongue Father God. Let them feel the impact of these prayers. Cover them with Your power and presence today. Amen.

Reflection Verses:

"May God be gracious to us and bless us and make His face shine on us—so that Your ways may be known on earth, Your salvation among all nations." – Psalm 67:1-2 NIV

Action: Intentional Prayer

Take 10-15 minutes to connect with Jesus about the people who matter most to you. Think about what they're going through right now. Do they know Jesus? How is your relationship with them?

Use this time to pray blessings over their lives and ask God how you can support and uplift them. Let this be a moment to ignite hope, encouragement, and love. As you pray, listen for God's guidance and jot down any thoughts or insights that come to mind.

Remember, your prayers can have a powerful impact! Share these encouraging words and blessings with your loved ones when the opportunity arises. Your support could make a world of difference in their lives!

NOTES

Faith In Action

WEEK 35

Seeing God In Everyday Moments

Today, pray that God would reveal Himself to you. Look around. You'll find Him in your reflection, your relationships, and the needs of those around you. God is right there in the small moments—when you choose kindness, serve others, or step outside your comfort zone. Seek Him with everything you've got, and you'll see Him moving in and through your life.

Reflection Verse:

"You will seek me and find me when you seek me with all your heart." —Jeremiah 29:13 NIV

Action: Reflect and Serve with Purpose

Take a moment to look in the mirror. Ask Jesus to show you how much you've grown. Be real with yourself—not to boost your ego, but to recognize the good God has done in your life and where you can grow even more. Reflect on who you used to be, who you are now, and who you are becoming. Celebrate the progress and give the unfinished parts to Him.

Then, pray for God to show you a way to make a difference today. It might be as simple as offering encouragement, helping a friend, or meeting a need you notice. Be ready to act—whether that's opening your schedule, giving time, or using what you have to help someone else. When you feel that nudge from God, go for it. You never know how one small act of kindness could be exactly what someone else needs. And when you show up, God shows up.

Seeing God In Everyday Moments

<u>NOTES</u>

WEEK 36
Affirmed By God

Today, pray that you experience the deep affirmation that only God can give. His approval isn't based on your performance or the opinions of others—it comes straight from His heart. When you let God's truth sink in, it can change how you see yourself and your day. May His thoughts fill your mind, giving you peace and reminding you that His presence is with you.

Reflection Verse:

"For it is not the one who commends himself who is approved, but the one whom the Lord commends." – 2 Corinthians 10:18

Action: Quiet Reflection and Prayer

No matter where you are in life—whether you feel close to God or distant—ask Him this question: "God, how do You see me?" Find a quiet place where you can sit for 5 to 10 minutes without distractions. Let yourself slow down and listen. Pay attention to anything that comes to mind—whether it's a verse, a song, or a gentle reminder from God.

If you notice any false ideas or broken thoughts about yourself, let Him speak truth into those areas. Stop striving to earn approval and just receive the love He's already offering you. God's affirmation isn't earned—it's freely given. Let that truth fill you today and remind you: You are already seen, known, and loved by Him.

NOTES

Faith In Action

WEEK 37

Redeeming Anxiety

Today, pray that the fear, anxiety, and panic you've been struggling with will be transformed into fuel for hope—hope that burns bright and steady within you. May your heart be set on fire with renewed strength and peace through Jesus, the source of all hope. Amen.

Reflection Verses:

"We have this hope as an anchor for the soul, firm and secure. It enters the inner sanctuary behind the curtain, where our forerunner, Jesus, has entered on our behalf."— Hebrews 6:19-20 NIV

Action: Meditation on Hope

Jesus has entered God's presence on your behalf, standing before the Father and interceding for you right now. Think about that: Jesus is praying for you at this very moment. His love for you is your anchor, keeping you steady no matter what life throws your way. Take a few minutes to sit quietly with this truth. Breathe deeply, and as you do, reflect on how Jesus is actively working for your good. How does knowing He is praying for you change the way you face today's challenges? How should it shape your response to fear, disappointment, or even success? Ask the Holy Spirit to help you grasp this truth deeply—that Jesus's prayers are holding you secure, no matter what. As you carry this awareness with you, let hope take root in your heart and guide your thoughts and actions. You are not alone—He is with you, praying and leading you every step of the way.

NOTES

WEEK 38

Eyes To See

Pray that hope sparks new faith within you, igniting dreams and visions into reality. Let hope and faith fuel your journey, making you expectant for what's ahead. Trust that Christ is working in powerful ways as you walk in obedience to Him. Keep believing, keep moving, and watch what happens. Amen.

Reflection Verses:

"Pray in the Spirit on all occasions with all kinds of prayers and requests. With this in mind, be alert and always keep on praying for all the Lord's people. Pray also for me, that whenever I speak, words may be given to me so I will fearlessly make known the mystery of the gospel." – Ephesians 6:18-20 NIV

Action: Prayer for Others

Many believers around the world face pressure and persecution for holding on to their faith. Take a few minutes today to pray for them. If a specific place comes to mind, lift that country or group of people up in prayer. If not, pray for the global church, asking that God would give our brothers and sisters strength, hope, and faith to stay bold in sharing the gospel. Pray that these believers would feel God's presence, even in the darkest moments, and that they would remain faithful to His calling. Ask for their courage to grow, just as Paul asked for boldness to proclaim the message of Christ. As you pray for them, let their example inspire you to walk faithfully in your own life, knowing that your prayers matter.

NOTES

WEEK 39

Fighting The Good Fight

Ask God to guide you into a meaningful battle today. It might not look how you expect—so be open to unexpected opportunities to stand against darkness, bring hope, and encourage those who are struggling. Keep your eyes open for the broken and hurting, whether it's a stranger or someone close to you. Amen.

Reflection Verse:

"Do all that you have in mind," his armor-bearer said. "Go ahead; I am with you heart and soul." – 1 Samuel 14:7 NIV

Action: Reading and Service

After reflecting on this prayer and verse, take time to read 1 Samuel 14:1-15. Just like Jonathan's armor-bearer, tell Jesus, "I'm with You, wherever You lead." Spend 5 minutes in silence, asking the Holy Spirit to reveal people in your life who are weighed down by struggles or spiritual battles. Write their names down and pray for them. Then, look for ways to support or encourage them. This could mean a kind word, a text message, or offering practical help. Your prayers and actions are part of God's battle plan to push back the enemy's influence and bring light to those around you.

Faith isn't just about avoiding evil—it's about confronting it with love, hope, and truth. Stay close to Christ, and step into the fight with boldness, knowing He's leading the way.

NOTES

Faith In Action

WEEK 40
Being Mindful Of Our Words And Actions

Today, ask God to reveal areas of your life you might not notice—things that unintentionally hurt others or block them from seeing God's work in you. Be ready for this truth to come from someone who challenges or frustrates you. Often, those uncomfortable moments reveal the blind spots we didn't know we had. Let's pray for God's help to see ourselves clearly and grow through these moments. Amen.

Reflection Verse:

"Though I am free and belong to no one, I have made myself a slave to everyone, to win as many as possible." – 1 Corinthians 9:19 NIV

Action: Silence and Journaling

The message of the Gospel isn't about us—our comfort, opinions, or image. It's about Jesus and sharing His love with others, especially those who think or live differently from us. Spend 5 to 10 minutes in silence, asking God to show you if you've prioritized being right over being loving. Have your words or actions unintentionally hurt others, even when you had good intentions?

While standing for truth matters, how we do it is just as important. After this quiet time, jot down what God reveals to you. Pray for wisdom to approach conversations with love and humility, and ask for grace to honor Christ in all your interactions.

Being Mindful Of Our Words And Actions

NOTES

FAITH IN ACTION

WEEK 41

Strength For Today

Pray that strength flows into every part of who you are—your mind, body, and spirit. May Jesus fill you with the energy and endurance you need for today. His strength isn't just for you to keep—it moves through you, helping you face challenges and lift others up. Take hold of it. Let it empower you. Amen.

Reflection Verses:

"I lift up my eyes to the mountains—where does my help come from? My help comes from the Lord, the Maker of heaven and earth." —Psalm 121:1-2 NIV

Action: Worship

Spend 10 to 15 minutes focusing on God. Put on some worship music, or read Scripture out loud. Praise Him for being your strength and for holding everything together. Remind yourself that it's God's power, not your own, that carries you through life. Let His strength refresh you and fill you with peace, knowing that you are supported by the One who created everything.

NOTES

WEEK 42
A Blessing Just For You

Today, pray that you realize how deeply God has blessed you. Imagine the Creator of everything—Heaven, Earth, and all that's good—looking right at you with love and favor. He notices you, cares about you, and has something amazing in store for you. Be ready. Stay open to what He wants to do in your life today because He's moving toward you, offering you more than you can imagine. Receive it fully. Amen.

Reflection Verse:

"Praise be to the God and Father of our Lord Jesus Christ, who has blessed us in the heavenly realms with every spiritual blessing in Christ."— Ephesians 1:3 NIV

Action: Prayer and Reflection

Today, remind yourself that you are chosen, seen, and loved by God. You don't need to be perfect for Him to smile at you—His love for you is beyond anything this world can offer. Spend a few minutes in prayer, asking God to show you how He's blessing you right now. Reflect on the fact that His love is constant, even when you feel like you don't deserve it. Rest in His delight for you, knowing that you are always seen, always loved, and never forgotten by Him.

NOTES

WEEK 43
The Desires Of Your Heart

Today, pray that God aligns your deepest desires with His plans for you. When what you want lines up with His heart, amazing things can happen. May God be your greatest desire today, and may He reveal the good things He has prepared just for you. Trust that His timing is perfect. Amen.

Reflection Verses:

"Trust in the Lord and do good; dwell in the land and enjoy safe pasture. Take delight in the Lord, and He will give you the desires of your heart." — Psalm 37:3-4 NIV

Action: Prayer and Journaling

God made you to experience joy and fulfillment, but real happiness comes from staying connected to Him. Take some time today to ask God about His plans for your life. Sometimes, what He wants might involve challenges, growth, or patience. But these tough moments often bring us closer to understanding who He is and how much He loves us.

Spend a few minutes in prayer, listening for His voice. Write down what you sense He wants for you—whether that's a new path, relationship, or personal growth. If you're comfortable, share these thoughts with a trusted friend or mentor. Stay open to God's guidance and trust that the best is yet to come.

NOTES

Faith In Action

WEEK 44

Experiencing God's Presence Everywhere

My Prayer for You:

I pray that you feel God's presence with you today—whether you're at home, in the car, at school, or sharing a meal. May His presence surround you throughout the day, giving you confidence that His plans are unfolding in your life.

Reflection Verses:

"Again, truly I tell you, if two of you agree on earth about anything you ask, it will be done by my Father in heaven. For where two or three gather in my name, I am there with them."
—Matthew 18:19-20 NIV

Activity: Prayer and Connection

Jesus reminds us that He is with us personally, but we can also experience Him more deeply when we connect with others. If you can, reach out to a friend or fellow believer today. Share what's going on in your lives and pray together, asking God to make His presence real in both of your experiences.

Experiencing God's Presence Everywhere

NOTES

WEEK 45
Jesus Is Alive And Working In You

Encouragement for Today:

Know with confidence that Jesus is alive and actively working in your life right now. Pray that you'll clearly see how He is moving in your circumstances. Remember, you are important to God's plan—valued, needed, and uniquely placed to make a difference exactly where you are. Be encouraged today!

Reflection Verse:

"But you are a chosen people, a royal priesthood, a holy nation, God's special possession, that you may declare the praises of him who called you out of darkness into his wonderful light." – 1 Peter 2:9 NIV

Activity: Memorization and Reflection

Take time to say 1 Peter 2:9 aloud, starting with your name: "[Your Name], you are a chosen person..." If you have a mirror nearby, look yourself in the eyes as you repeat it. Let these words remind you of your identity in God. Try to memorize the verse and repeat it in the morning when you wake up and at night before you sleep, keeping God's truth close to your heart.

NOTES

Faith In Action

WEEK 46

Thinking And Living Like Jesus

Encouragement for Today:

I pray that today you realize you have the mind of Christ. May your thoughts, actions, love, and responses reflect Jesus. As you do, watch how things around you change. May God's will be done through you in the places where you have influence.

Reflection Verse:

"But you will receive power when the Holy Spirit comes on you; and you will be my witnesses in Jerusalem, and in all Judea and Samaria, and to the ends of the earth." – Acts 1:8 NIV

Activity: Prayer and Self-Reflection

Pray and ask the Holy Spirit to help you represent Jesus in your world. Take a moment to reflect on where your thoughts or actions haven't aligned with Jesus. Write those down, ask for forgiveness, and pray for change. At the end of the day, review how you were able to reflect Christ's love and where you could improve. Use this to grow closer to Him each day.

NOTES

FAITH IN ACTION

WEEK 47

Managing Your Time With God's Help

Prayer for Today:

Jesus, I feel overwhelmed by everything I need to get done. As I try to plan, time seems to slip away, leaving me stressed. You are not limited by time, and you have control over it. Please guide my thoughts and help me manage my time wisely. Organize my schedule, make my efforts meaningful, and help me focus on what really matters. Thank You for walking with me through it all. May Your will be done today. Amen.

Reflection Verse:

"May the favor of the Lord our God rest on us; establish the work of our hands—yes, establish the work of our hands." – Psalm 90:17 NIV

Activity: Journaling and Prayer

Take a few minutes to write down everything on your mind—tasks, deadlines, worries, or plans. Once it's all on paper, pray over each item, one by one, giving them to God. Remember, if you've given your life to Christ, that includes your schedule too. Ask Him to show you what to prioritize and listen for His guidance. Let His peace replace any anxiety about time.

NOTES

Faith In Action

WEEK 48
Overcoming Fear With God's Power

Pray that God removes the fears that have been weighing you down. Don't fear people—they don't hold real power over you. Don't fear sickness—Jesus is in control of all things. Don't fear losing money—it all belongs to Him. Don't fear failure or not being enough—you are more than a conqueror through the love of Christ. Even fear of success or the devil has no place in your life. You are a child of God, and fear doesn't get to rule over you. Let God's peace fill your heart and mind today.

Reflection Verse:

"For the Spirit God gave us does not make us timid, but gives us power, love, and self-discipline." – 2 Timothy 1:7 NIV

Activity: Memorization and Practice

Read today's verse out loud several times until you memorize it. Find a small object, like a rock or keychain, and keep it with you throughout the week. Whenever you see or touch it, remind yourself of this verse by repeating it in your mind or aloud. Speak this truth not only over yourself but also into the lives of friends who are struggling with fear. Let God's Word replace fear with His power and peace in your mind.

NOTES

FAITH IN ACTION

WEEK 49
Replacing Fear With God's Peace

Prayer for Today:

Lord God, I know that fear has no place in Your presence. I ask that Your powerful presence remove any fears that try to creep in today. Help me experience You in a real way and remind me that fear is nothing but a lie. Thank You, Holy Spirit, for filling me with peace and security.

Reflection Verse:

"For the Spirit God gave us does not make us timid, but gives us power, love, and self-discipline." – 2 Timothy 1:7 NIV

Activity: Pray for Others

Think of someone in your life who struggles with fear. How well do they know God? Pray that God will become so real to them that they won't be able to ignore His presence. Ask God to remove their fears, doubts, and insecurities in Jesus' name. Read today's verse as a prayer over their situation and thank God for working in their life.

NOTES

Faith In Action

Week 50
Choosing Selflessness

Prayer for Today:

Jesus, help me break free from selfish thoughts and actions. I don't want to use people for my own benefit. Instead, help me see them as valuable and precious, made in Your image. Teach me to honor, encourage, and care for others today. Show me how to reflect Your love in my relationships. Amen.

Reflection Verse:

"Sitting down, Jesus called the Twelve and said, 'Anyone who wants to be first must be the very last, and the servant of all.'" –Mark 9:35 NIV

Activity: Focus on Others

One of the best ways to overcome selfishness is by focusing on other people's needs and dreams. In Mark 9, the disciples argued about who was the greatest, and Jesus reminded them that greatness comes through serving others.

Take some time today to pray for two or three people. These could be friends, family members, or even people you struggle to get along with. Find a small object—a rock, ring, or bracelet—that you can keep with you. Every time you touch or notice it, pray for those people and ask God how you can encourage or help them. When you're around others today, take a moment to notice their needs and ask God how you can be a blessing. Then take action.

NOTES

Faith In Action

WEEK 51
Following God's Guidance

Prayer for Today:

Lord, please fill me with Your Spirit and guide my steps today. Lead me where You want me to go. Help me notice what You want me to see and say what You want me to say. Let me hear what You want me to hear, rest when I need to rest, and pray when You call me to pray. Direct every part of my day, Lord. Amen.

Reflection Verses:

"For none of us lives for ourselves alone, and none of us dies for ourselves alone. If we live, we live for the Lord; and if we die, we die for the Lord. So, whether we live or die, we belong to the Lord."– Romans 14:7-8 NIV

Activity: Silence and Reflection

These words remind us that everything we do should be for God's glory. Take 5-10 minutes to sit quietly without distractions. Reflect on your day ahead and ask God to guide your priorities. Is there anything He wants to shift in your schedule? Are there areas where you haven't put Him first? Does He want to remind you of His love for you? Spend time listening to His voice, and carry that sense of His direction with you throughout the day.

NOTES

Faith In Action

WEEK 52
God's Life-Giving Breath

Prayer for Today:

May God breathe life into my heart and soul today. Let His breath fill every part of me, bringing life to areas that feel empty or broken. May those hurting places be restored, healed and renewed. Right now, I receive His life, His breath, and His hope. God, breathe on us all. Amen".

Reflection Verse:

"*The Spirit of God has made me; the breath of the Almighty gives me life.*" –Job 33:4 NIV

Activity: Memorization and Reflection

After reading the prayer, memorize Job 33:4. For the next three days, carry a small item—like a rock or a coin—in your pocket or backpack. Every time you notice it, remind yourself of the new life Christ has given you through His resurrection. Take a moment to reflect on that truth with the Holy Spirit and ask Him to make it real in your everyday experience.

NOTES

Faith In Action

BONUS WEEK 1

Living In God's Grace

Prayer for Today: Lord, I know I don't deserve Your grace, yet You give it to me freely. Help me never act like I'm entitled to it because I'm not. Your grace is beyond my understanding—how can a perfect God love someone as imperfect as me? Thank You for this incredible gift. Teach me to receive it humbly and share it generously with others. Jesus, You are the ultimate expression of God's grace. Amen.

Reflection Verses:

"For the grace of God has appeared that offers salvation to all people. It teaches us to say 'No' to ungodliness and worldly passions, and to live self-controlled, upright, and godly lives in this present age, while we wait for the blessed hope—the appearing of the glory of our great God and Savior, Jesus Christ, who gave himself for us to redeem us from all wickedness and to purify for himself a people that are his very own, eager to do what is good." – Titus 2:11-14 NIV

Activity: Worship and Living with Grace

God's grace saves us—not because of anything we've done, but simply because He loves us. While we can't earn this gift, understanding it changes how we live. Now, we do good not to gain salvation, but because we belong to Him. During your devotional time today, reflect on the prayer and think about who God is. Take a moment to worship Him in awe for His grace. Then, as you go about your day, commit to live with that grace. Be kind, patient, and forgiving toward others, letting His grace influence how you treat those around you.

NOTES

About The Author

Teejay was born in Poplar Bluff, Missouri, as the baby of 6 children. As a child, he saw his mother be miraculously healed from paralyzation and his father be delivered from a drug and alcohol addiction. He grew up knowing that he was called into ministry, but stayed in and out of trouble and tried to run from his calling. He graduated from Mineral Area College and Missouri Southern State University as a multi-sport All-American athlete, with degrees in Criminal Justice and Law Enforcement, but decided to pursue a career in education and accepted a position as the Director of an alternative school in Miami, Oklahoma.

After 3 years with the school, Teejay finally accepted his call into full-time ministry. Teejay is a 5 sport professional athlete (Track, Basketball, MMA, Boxing, Kickboxing) and uses his athletic background as a platform to "Bring hope to the hurting, no matter the cost." His heart is to let people know that God loves them, has a plan for them, and can use them for His good no matter what they have done or been through. As an Evangelist and Motivational Speaker, Teejay has been sharing encouragement and the love of Jesus across the globe in schools, colleges, professional teams, churches, business meetings, and conferences for almost 10 years. Teejay and his wife, Britney, have 5 kids (Joseph, Aria, Jacob, Ty and Kyrie). They live in Missouri, where they founded and operate Mo Legacy, a sports ministry program.

www.ingramcontent.com/pod-product-compliance
Lightning Source LLC
LaVergne TN
LVHW061047070526
838201LV00074B/5211